mummy
& me
craft

DK

LONDON, NEW YORK, MUNICH,
MELBOURNE, and DELHI

Senior designer Hannah Moore
Editor Jo Casey
Photographer Dave King
Production editor Andy Hilliard
Production controller Ché Creasey
Jacket designer Rosie Levine
Managing editor Penny Smith
Managing art editor Marianne Markham
Creative director Jane Bull
Category publisher Mary Ling

First published in Great Britain in 2014 by
Dorling Kindersley Limited
80 Strand, London WC2R 0RL

Copyright © 2014 Dorling Kindersley

A Penguin Random House Company

10 9 8 7 6 5 4 3 2 1
001-196500-02/14

A CIP catalogue record for this book
is available from the British Library.

ISBN: 978-1-4093-3846-8

Printed and bound in China
by Hung Hing

Contents

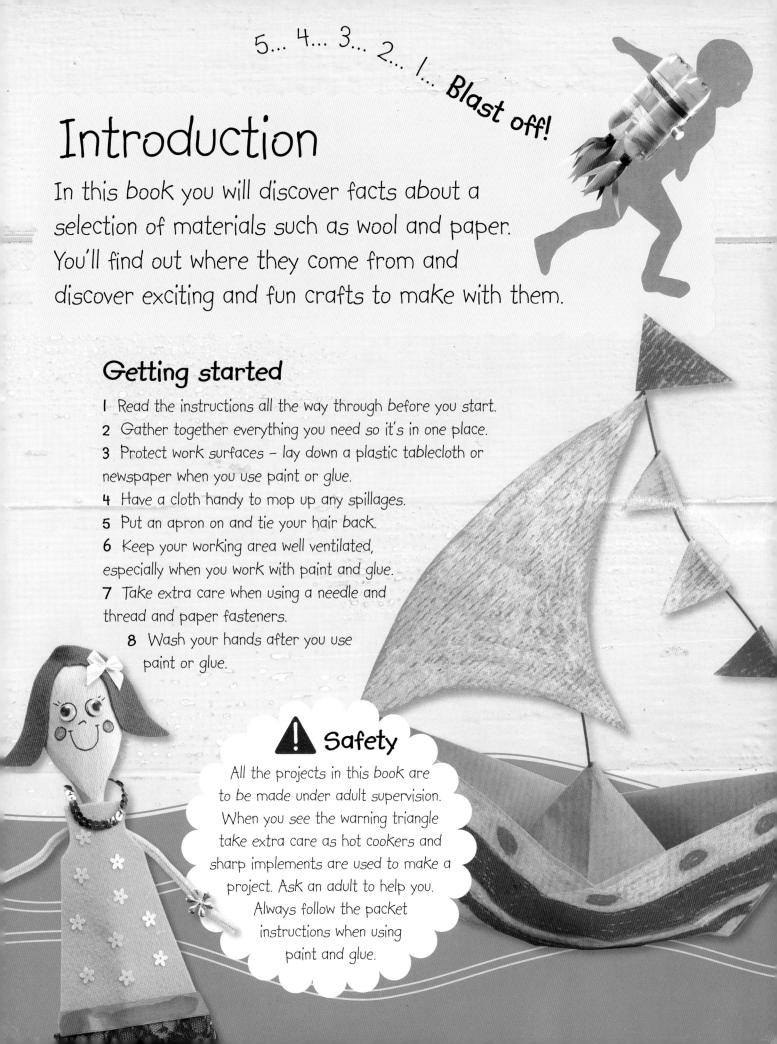

5... 4... 3... 2... 1... Blast off!

Introduction

In this book you will discover facts about a selection of materials such as wool and paper. You'll find out where they come from and discover exciting and fun crafts to make with them.

Getting started

1 Read the instructions all the way through before you start.

2 Gather together everything you need so it's in one place.

3 Protect work surfaces – lay down a plastic tablecloth or newspaper when you use paint or glue.

4 Have a cloth handy to mop up any spillages.

5 Put an apron on and tie your hair back.

6 Keep your working area well ventilated, especially when you work with paint and glue.

7 Take extra care when using a needle and thread and paper fasteners.

8 Wash your hands after you use paint or glue.

⚠ Safety

All the projects in this book are to be made under adult supervision. When you see the warning triangle take extra care as hot cookers and sharp implements are used to make a project. Ask an adult to help you. Always follow the packet instructions when using paint and glue.

Paper is pretty amazing. You can use it to make lots of fun crafts; from beads and boats, to windmills and windsocks!

What is paper?

We use paper to write on, paint on, draw on, and so much more. But have you ever thought about where paper comes from? Paper as we know it doesn't grow on trees but it is made from trees!

Paper can be **recycled**, which means turning something old into something new.

Recycled paper can be shaped into lots of paper products, like egg boxes. (Turn to pages 50-51 for a brilliant egg box craft!)

Think about how many times you use paper every day. Newspaper, tissue paper, wrapping paper, toilet paper, cards, magazines, comics, books, money, tracing paper, maps, sweet wrappers... paper is everywhere!

How is paper made?

Trees

Trees are cut down and the branches are cut off.

Paper mill

At the paper mill the bark is removed from the logs. The logs are crushed into a mushy pulp and water and chemicals are added.

The water is squeezed from the pulp and then the pulp is rolled flat into paper. The rolls of paper are cut into smaller rolls, ready to be delivered to shops.

Before the invention of paper, people used stones, animal skins, palm leaves, or fabric to write on.

Huge rolls of paper

Paper was invented a long time ago by the ancient Egyptians. They made it from the papyrus plant, which is where paper gets its name.

Larry the lion mask

Grab a paper plate, yellow paint, and coloured card to make a Larry the lion mask. It's pretty easy to make, just follow the steps and you'll be roaring like a lion in no time!

Ask an adult to help you cut out the templates on page 78.

A female lion is called a lioness. A lioness doesn't have a mane so don't add raffia ribbon to the edges if you want to make a lioness mask.

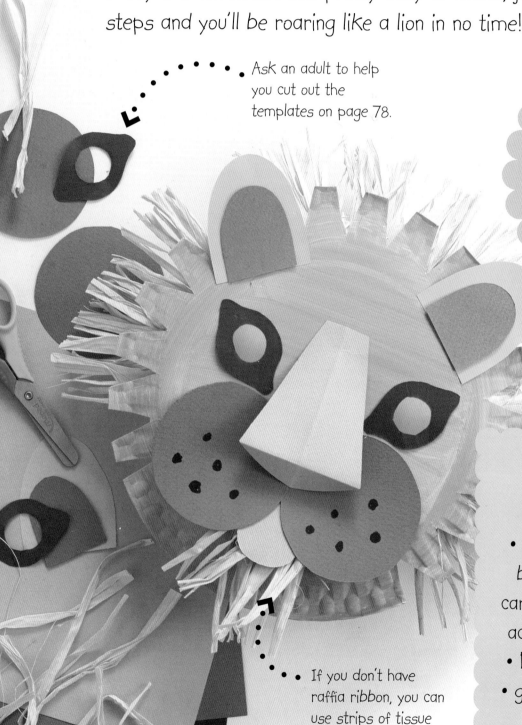

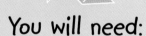

You will need:

tracing paper • pencil • scissors • yellow, beige, brown, and dark brown card • paper plate • yellow acrylic paint • paintbrush • PVA glue • raffia ribbon • glue stick • black felt-tip pen • elastic

If you don't have raffia ribbon, you can use strips of tissue paper instead.

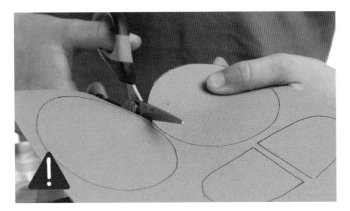

1 Trace the templates on page 78 onto tracing paper and cut them out. Place the shapes over card, draw around them, and cut them out.

2 Paint the back of the paper plate yellow and leave to dry. Cut small triangles ³/₄ of the way around the edges of the plate.

3 Position the eyes on the plate and trace around the circles in the middle. Ask an adult to carefully cut out the two circles.

4 Cut strips of raffia ribbon and glue them ³/₄ of the way around the edges of the plate. Glue strips of raffia onto the bottom of the plate.

5 To make the nose, fold the widest end under by about 1cm (½in). Fold in half lengthways and then open it out.

6 Draw dots on the cheeks and then glue the ears, eyes, chin, cheeks, and the shortest end of the nose onto the plate.

7 Ask an adult to cut two holes in both sides of the plate. Thread elastic through the holes and tie the ends.

More animal masks

You can make all sorts of animal masks. Would you like to be an exotic bird or a bouncing bunny? Let your imagination go wild!

If you haven't got feathers you can use coloured tissue paper to make this bright bird mask. Your mask doesn't have to be round – experiment with different shapes.

You can attach your mask to a stick if you haven't got any elastic to tie it around your head.

You need two paper plates, felt, raffia ribbon, white paper, and a pom-pom to make this cute bunny. (Use a ready-made pom-pom or make your own. See pages 26-27 for pom-pom instructions.)

Most origami starts with a square piece of paper.

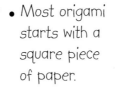

Origami windmill

Wow your friends with this fabulous origami windmill. Pin it to a stick, take it outside, and watch it whirl in the wind.

You will need:

colourful square paper • scissors • stick • drawing pin

Origami is the Japanese art of folding paper to make shapes.

Use sweet wrappers to make these cute mini windmills.

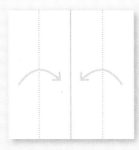

1 Fold the square piece of paper in half and unfold.

2 Fold both sides into the middle.

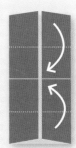

3 Fold the rectangle in half, crease, and unfold. Bring the top and bottom into the middle and fold.

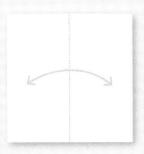

4 Fold the bottom right corner to the top left corner to make a triangle, and unfold. Repeat with the bottom left corner. Unfold the square to make a rectangle.

5 With your forefingers inside the bottom corners, your remaining fingers holding down the middle, and your thumbs underneath, gently pull the corners out, to make a boat shape.

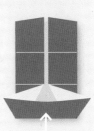

6 Press the middle down and crease well.

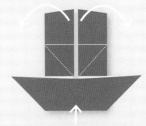

7 Repeat steps 5-6 to the top corners.

8 Fold the bottom left triangle shape down and then fold the top right corner triangle shape up.

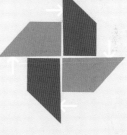

9 Poke your fingers inside each of the four triangles to give them shape.

10 Cut one big circle and one small circle out of paper and place them in the middle of the windmill. Ask an adult to pin your windmill to a stick.

Blow on your windmill and watch it spin!

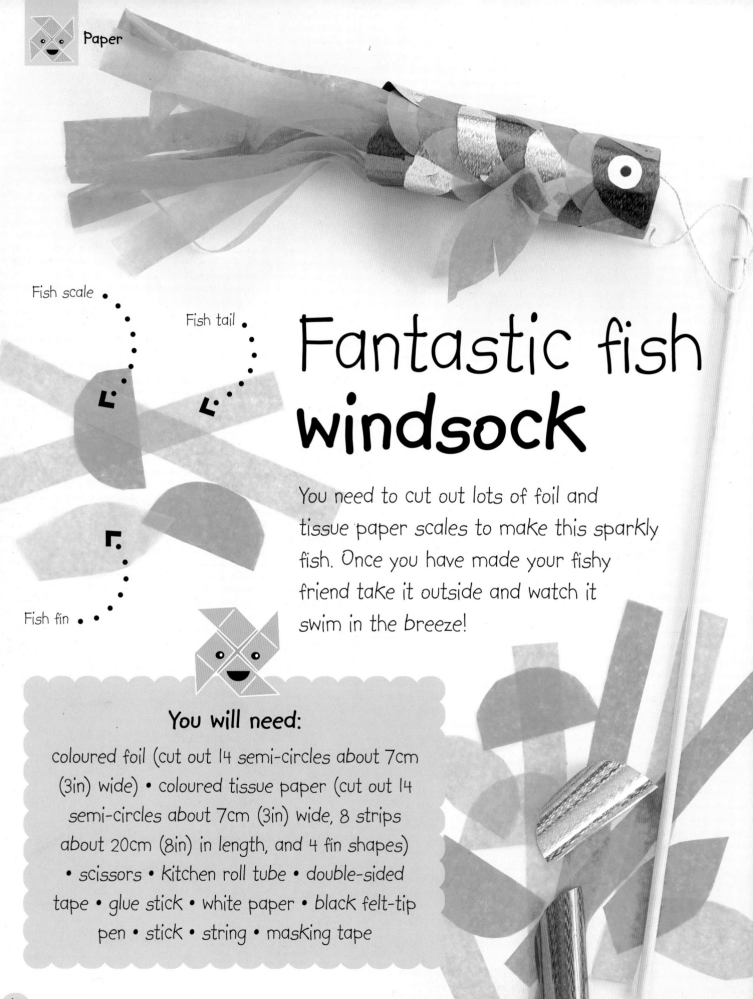

Fish scale

Fish tail

Fish fin

Fantastic fish
windsock

You need to cut out lots of foil and tissue paper scales to make this sparkly fish. Once you have made your fishy friend take it outside and watch it swim in the breeze!

You will need:

coloured foil (cut out 14 semi-circles about 7cm (3in) wide) • coloured tissue paper (cut out 14 semi-circles about 7cm (3in) wide, 8 strips about 20cm (8in) in length, and 4 fin shapes) • scissors • kitchen roll tube • double-sided tape • glue stick • white paper • black felt-tip pen • stick • string • masking tape

1 Ask an adult to cut a kitchen roll tube in half. Stick double-sided tape inside one end of the tube, all the way around.

2 Spread glue all around one end of the tube.

3 Stick the tissue paper and foil scales onto the tube, overlapping each scale slightly. Alternate between the tissue paper and the foil scales.

4 Continue spreading glue around the tube and sticking on the scales. Slightly overlap each row until the whole tube is covered.

5 For the fish eyes, draw two small circles onto white paper and cut them out. Draw a black dot in the middle of each circle and glue onto each side of the tube.

6 Stick the fish tails onto the tape inside the tail end of the tube. Then stick two fins onto each side of the tube.

You can also design your own windsock. Take plain paper and use colourful felt-tips, pencils, crayons, or paint to make a pattern. Glue the paper onto the tube.

Tie about 60cm (24in) of string around one end of a stick. Attach both ends of the string inside the top of the tube with masking tape. Then take your fish outside and watch it swim!

Pretty paper beads

Make one-of-a-kind jewellery by rolling triangles of paper into beads. Use a mixture of colours to make pretty necklaces and bracelets. Ready, steady, now get rolling!

Only use a little glue or your beads will stick to the knitting needle.

You can use old catalogues, posters, and wallpaper.

Coat your finished beads with varnish to make them shiny and strong.

You will need:

magazines, coloured paper, or wrapping paper • ruler • pencil • scissors • knitting needle or wooden skewer • glue stick • glitter glue • string • elastic • plastic beads

Before you cut out lots of triangles make one test bead with your chosen paper to see if you like the overall effect.

1 Use a ruler to measure out triangles about 3cm (1^{1}/$_{4}$in) wide and 30cm (12in) in length onto paper. Carefully cut out each triangle.

2 Place the needle on the widest end of the triangle and roll the paper around the needle twice. Spread glue along the rest of the triangle.

3 Continue rolling the needle to the end of the triangle, pressing down firmly as you roll.

4 Slide the bead off the needle and leave to dry. Before beginning your next bead wipe the needle (and your hands!) clean of glue.

5 Once your beads are dry, squirt a dollop of glitter glue onto scrap paper. Roll each bead in it to create a fabulous sparkly effect.

6 Once you start making paper beads it will be hard to stop! Make lots and then turn the page to find out how to make a fantastic bracelet.

You can add plastic beads to your necklaces and bracelets.

Make lots of necklaces in different lengths. Just thread your beads onto string and secure with a knot. Wear them all at once to make a real style statement!

Follow the steps on the right to make this beadtastic bracelet.

Beadtastic bracelet

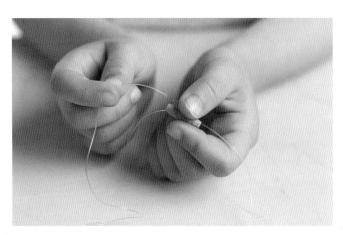

1 Fold a length of elastic in half and check that it will fit around your wrist. Thread one end through one side of a bead and thread the other end through the opposite side of the bead.

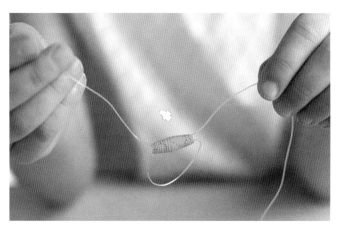

2 Pull both ends of elastic until the bead reaches the end of the loop.

3 Continue adding beads onto the elastic in this way. Stop when you are near the end of the elastic.

4 To finish, thread one end of elastic through the first bead you started off with. Then thread the other end of elastic through the opposite side of the same bead. Tie the ends in a double knot to secure it.

Homemade paste

If you don't have wallpaper paste you can make your own. Ask an adult to follow the steps below. You will need 1 cup of plain flour and 3 cups of water.

1 Put 1 cup of water and 1 cup of flour into a saucepan and stir until the mixture is smooth.

2 Add the rest of the water and bring to the boil, stirring all the time.

3 Pour the mixture into a bowl and leave to cool.

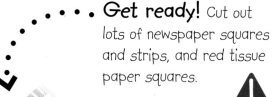

Ollie the **octopus**

Use old newspapers to make new things, like Ollie the papier mâché octopus. Octopuses usually live in the ocean, but Ollie will be more than happy to live in your bedroom!

You will need:

scissors • newspapers • red tissue paper • inflated balloon • masking tape • jar • petroleum jelly • paintbrush • homemade paste or wallpaper paste • garden wire • white paper • black felt-tip pen • PVA glue • blue tissue paper (cut out about 60 small circles)

Get ready! Cut out lots of newspaper squares and strips, and red tissue paper squares.

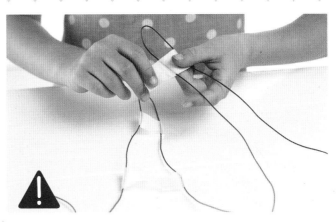

1 Tape the *balloon* on top of the jar and smooth petroleum jelly all over it. Use the brush to paste on the newspaper squares, and continue pasting them on until you have about four layers.

2 Put the *balloon* aside to dry. Ask an adult to cut 8 pieces of garden wire about 25cm (10in) long and shape into tentacles. Use masking tape to hold the tentacle shapes in place.

3 Attach the tentacles to the *balloon* with masking tape. Then, brush the newspaper strips with paste. Wrap them around each tentacle, until they are all covered.

4 Next, paste the tissue paper squares all over the *balloon* and tentacles, until it is completely covered.

Stick the eyes onto Ollie.

5 For the eyes, cut two oval shapes about 10cm (4in) long and 7cm (3in) wide from white paper. Colour in black pupils.

6 Glue the tissue paper circles all over the balloon and tentacles. Set aside to dry.

7 You're almost finished! Turn the balloon upside down, snip the knot, and remove the balloon.

21

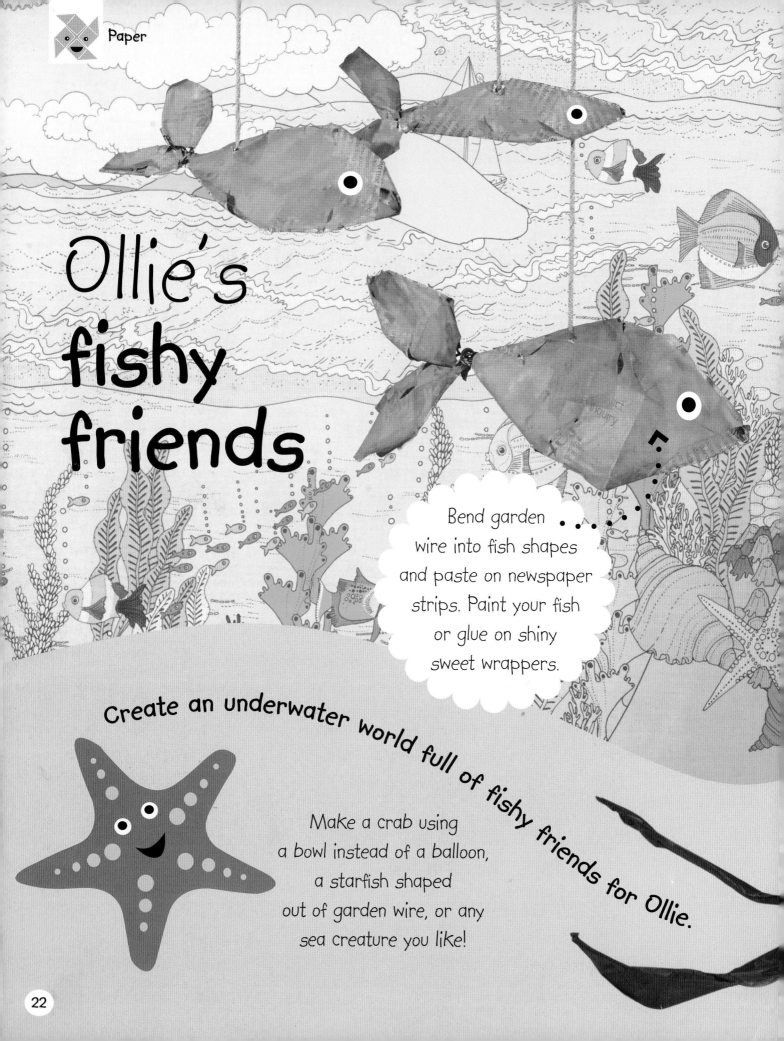

Ollie's fishy friends

Bend garden wire into fish shapes and paste on newspaper strips. Paint your fish or glue on shiny sweet wrappers.

Create an underwater world full of fishy friends for Ollie.

Make a crab using a bowl instead of a balloon, a starfish shaped out of garden wire, or any sea creature you like!

⚠ Ask an adult to make a hole through the top of Ollie. Thread wool through the hole at the bottom and out of the hole at the top and hang Ollie from a shelf.

Magazines, comic books, sweet wrappers, junk mail, and envelopes can all be used to make a papier mâché project!

Female sheep are called ewes and males are called rams. Baby sheep are called lambs.

What is Wool?

Wool comes from sheep and has been used for thousands of years to make clothes that keep us warm and dry. It is very clever stuff – water runs off it and it's difficult to set on fire, making it a useful material in firefighter's clothes.

Up to eight woolly jumpers can be made from one fleece (a sheep's coat).

You won't find a sheep with a bright pink fleece! Wool absorbs dye easily and can be dyed into beautiful colours.

Wool is good for the planet because it is biodegradable. This means that it can be broken down easily without harming the environment.

A good shearer might take less than **five minutes to shear a sheep**.

Every spring, sheep have a dramatic haircut and their fleeces are shorn off. The fleece is removed in one single piece by a shearer. The shearer must hold a sheep in place and not cut the sheep's skin.

The wool is washed to remove any stains and then it goes through a carding machine, which combs the wool to remove all the dirt.

Raw wool is soft and fluffy!

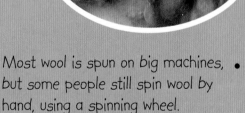

Most wool is spun on big machines, but some people still spin wool by hand, using a spinning wheel.

A modern factory spinning machine pulls and twists the wool tightly into long strands, called yarn. Then it's ready for knitting!

Wool can be the natural colour of the sheep it came from, or it can be dyed to any colour.

Fluffy pom-poms

Make these cute balls of fluff by using scraps of wool that are too short for knitting. Creating these pom-poms is so satisfying that chances are once you make one you simply won't be able to stop!

Get ready! Cut two matching discs of card with holes in the middle. Then cut slits through the edges, like these ones.

You will need:

card • pencil • scissors • wool • fabric glue • mini pom-poms • googly eyes

The size of your discs determines the size of your pom-pom. About 10cm (4in) wide is a good size.

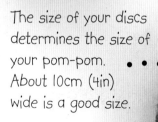

1 Put one cardboard disc on top of the other and tie the end of the wool around them.

2 Wind the wool around and around the discs, through the middle and over the top. The more wool you use, the fatter your pom-pom will be.

3 Slip the scissors between the discs and carefully snip the wool all the way around, holding the discs firmly.

4 Wrap a piece of wool between the discs. Pull the wool tightly and tie in a knot to hold the wool in place.

5 Gently pull the discs off the pom-pom. Trim off the ends of the long piece of wool.

6 Fluff up your pom-pom and snip all around it to neaten it up. Stick down mini pom-poms and googly eyes to finish off your pom-pom.

Pom-pom creatures

You can craft your pom-poms into all manner of weird and wonderful creatures. Just gather together felt, googly eyes, and cardboard and get creating!

Squeak, squeak! Plait strands of wool to make a tail for this sweet pom-pom mouse.

Stick a small pom-pom onto a bigger pom-pom with fabric glue to make this cute bunny.

If you don't have any felt use coloured card instead. Cut out the shapes and use craft glue to stick them on.

Use colourful feathers to make this adorable pom-pom bird.

Create a monster pom-pom using a pipe cleaner for antennae and felt for feet.

Paper plate weaving

Use a paper plate and scraps of colourful wool to make a wonderful weave. Your finished weave can be used as a colourful coaster, a pretty wall hanging, or it can be placed in a frame.

If you don't have an embroidery needle you can use a large paper clip instead.

You can also use string, plastic bags, and old T-shirts cut into strips to weave with!

You will need:
paper plate
• pencil • ruler
• scissors • skewer
• embroidery needle
• wool

When you have finished weaving, cut each strand and tie them in a knot.

A paper plate in any size will do.

A plastic drink stirrer can also be used to weave with.

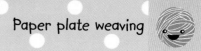

1 Use a ruler to divide the plate into 16 equal segments. Carefully cut out 16 triangle shapes all around the edge of the plate.

2 Ask an adult to carefully make a hole in the middle of the plate with a skewer. Then thread wool through the hole from behind.

3 Hook the wool over a segment and back under through the hole. Repeat this on all the segments and then tie a knot at the back.

4 Cut a short piece of wool and tie two of the strands together to make 15 segments. Now you're ready to weave!

5 Thread a needle with wool and thread it through the hole from behind. Place the needle under a strand, then over the next strand. Continue to thread over and under, all around the plate.

6 To change wool colour, tie the end of the new piece of wool onto the end of the last piece of wool you used. Tuck the strands under the weave. When you've covered the plate, tie the end of the wool to a strand and tuck it under your weave.

Scale it up!

Take weaving to another level by using a hula hoop. Chunky wool works best for a massive weave – double up each piece of wool to make it even chunkier and then get weaving!

under

over

under

over

under

over

Your finished hula hoop weave can be used as a comfy rug or you can make two and stitch them together to make a cushion cover – it will brighten up any room!

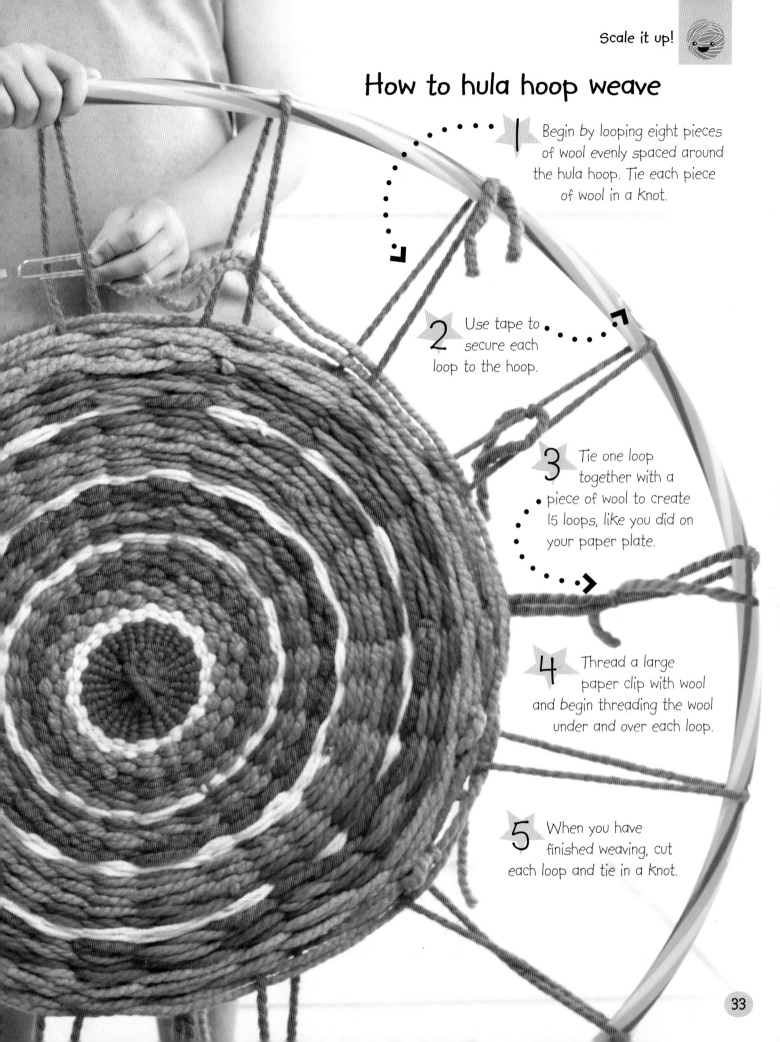

How to hula hoop weave

1 Begin by looping eight pieces of wool evenly spaced around the hula hoop. Tie each piece of wool in a knot.

2 Use tape to secure each loop to the hoop.

3 Tie one loop together with a piece of wool to create 15 loops, like you did on your paper plate.

4 Thread a large paper clip with wool and begin threading the wool under and over each loop.

5 When you have finished weaving, cut each loop and tie in a knot.

Wool

The stitching is done on these pegs.

Any colourful wool will do, but try using up leftover wool – it's perfect for making long, stripey cord.

Knitting doll

This clever doll is very good at knitting. With your help she produces lovely cord that can be made into beautiful things for you and your friends.

Use a knitting pin to lift the wool over the pegs.

As if by magic, gorgeous knitted cord comes out of the bottom of the doll.

You will need:

colourful wool • knitting doll
• knitting pin • scissors

34

1 Thread the wool down through the centre of the doll, leaving about 10cm (4in) of wool out of the bottom. Wrap the wool around the first peg.

2 Then wrap the wool around the second, third, and the fourth peg.

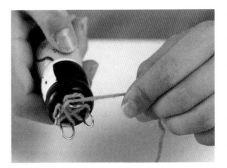

3 Lay the wool across the outside of the first peg.

4 Now you're ready to knit! Use the knitting pin to pull out the bottom loop from the first peg.

5 Lift the loop over the peg and the stitch is complete. Continue to lay the wool across the outside of each peg and lift each stitch over it.

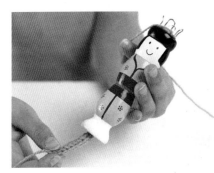

6 Pull on the wool at the end as you complete each stitch. Slowly, the knitted cord will appear out of the bottom of the doll.

Casting off

1 Lift the last stitch you made onto the peg next to it, pull out the bottom loop, and lift the loop over the peg.

2 Repeat step one until just one loop is left.

3 Lift up the loop with your pin and enlarge it with the pin.

4 To finish, cut the thread, pass it through the loop, and pull it tight. Tie a knot to secure it.

Cute creations

You won't get bored making cute creations with your knitted cord. Purses, petals, or pen jars – you can make plenty of things!

Pen pot

Use up scraps of wool to knit long, colourful cord. Ask an adult to glue the cord around a glass jar. You can use your jazzed-up jar to put your paintbrushes and pencils in.

Coil flower

1 Roll about 11cm (4⅓in) of cord into a coil. Use pins to secure the coil shape and then stitch together at the back. Remove the pins after stitching.

2 For the petals, knit about 55cm (22in) of cord. Pin each petal shape to the coil and then stitch in place at the back. Remove the pins after stitching.

You can sew a brooch pin to the back of your flowers and pin them to a hat or a jacket.

Button flower

1 You will need to knit about 40cm (16in) of cord to make these button flowers. Fold the cord into a flower shape, using pins to hold the shape in place.

2 Stitch the petal shapes together at the back. Remove the pins after stitching.

3 Sew a bright button in the middle of your flower.

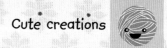

This purse is a project to do over time because you will need to knit lots and lots of cord to make it. You will be so pleased with the result all your work will have been worth it!

Sew on a button and a fastening loop to keep your things safe.

Pretty purse

1 Knit two pieces of cord about 160cm (63in) long. Roll one cord into a coil and use pins to hold the shape in place.

2 Stitch the coil together at the back. This will be on the inside of the purse. Remove the pins after stitching. Repeat with the other cord.

3 Place one unstitched side of a coil on top of the unstitched side of the other coil. Stitch them together around the edges, leaving the top unstitched. Turn the purse inside out, so that all the stitching is on the inside.

4 Knit another piece of cord for the strap. It can be as long or as short as you like. Place both ends of the cord inside the top of the bag and sew in place.

What is paint?

Imagine a world without paint – it would be a very dull place! People have been using paint to colour everything from caves, pictures, and buildings for thousands of years.

How is paint made?

The two main ingredients in paint are "pigment", which gives paint its colour, and "binder", which gives paint its texture. Pigment and binder are mixed together and then poured into a milling machine, which spreads the pigments evenly.

Pigments are crushed into a fine powder.

Start with some beautiful **pigments**...mix each pigment with **binder**...

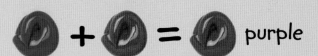

Red ochre is a natural pigment found on earth. Cavemen mixed it with dirt, saliva, or animal fat to create paint.

Cave paintings The first paintings were created on cave walls. Paintbrushes didn't exist so fingertips, moss, twigs, feathers, and hollow bones were used.

If you run out of your favourite paint, don't despair! Did you know that if you mix two primary colours (red, yellow, or blue) together it makes a completely different colour?

+ = purple

+ = orange

+ = green

...put the paint mixture into a **tube**...and then have **fun!**

Sticker
T-shirt

Masking
tape
T-shirt

Design a T-shirt

Take a plain T-shirt and transform it into a true
original. All you need is tape, stickers, paint,
and a bit of imagination!

Use stickers that have
interesting shapes,
like these stars.

Use a plain T-shirt
in any colour.

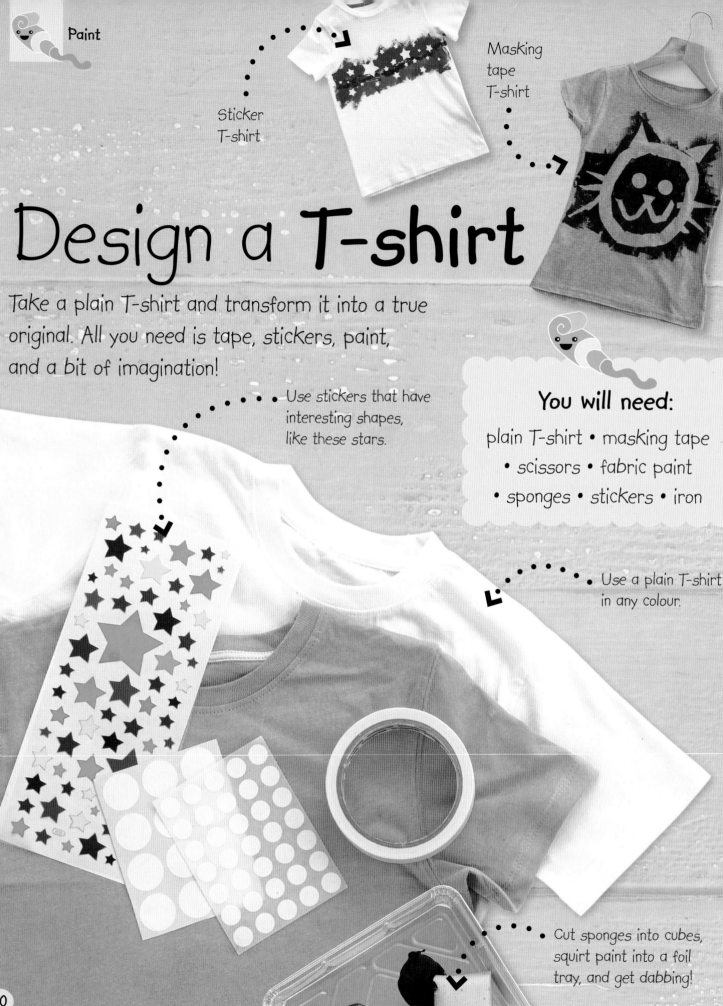

Cut sponges into cubes,
squirt paint into a foil
tray, and get dabbing!

Masking tape T-shirt

1 Lay the T-shirt flat and stick strips of masking tape onto the T-shirt in any design you like.

2 Dab fabric paint on and around the bits of masking tape with a sponge.

3 Leave the paint to dry and then carefully peel off the bits of masking tape.

4 Turn the T-shirt inside out and ask an adult to iron over the design to fix it in place.

Sticker T-shirt

1 Apply the stickers to the T-shirt in any way you like.

2 Dab fabric paint on and around the stickers with a sponge and leave to dry.

3 Peel off the stickers. Turn the T-shirt inside out and ask an adult to iron over the design.

Paint

If you are not
sure what design to
put on your T-shirt
you can experiment
on paper first.

A masking
tape or sticker
T-shirt makes a
great, original
present for a
special friend.

42

The big reveal!

Revealing the design on your new T-shirt is surprising, exciting, and lots of fun!

Make sure the paint has completely dried before you peel off the masking tape or stickers.

If you don't live near a beach, you can buy stones in most craft shops.

Painted stones

Transform stones into fabulous works of art! You can turn them into bugs or butterflies or cover them in patterns. Display them on your desk, shelves, or use them as paperweights.

Use fine felt-tip pens or paintbrushes to add details to your stones.

You will need:

clean, dry stones • acrylic paints • paintbrushes • clear varnish or PVA glue • felt-tip pens

Choose colourful acrylic paints, then get painting!

1 You can paint any design you like, but for a lovely ladybird follow these steps. Paint the stone all over with a *base* colour. Your design will really stand out on white paint.

2 Once the base paint is dry, paint three quarters of the stone red and leave to dry.

3 Paint the remainder of the stone black and add a black line down the middle. Don't forget to give your ladybird black spots, two white eyes with black dots in the middle, and a red smile!

4 When the paint is completely dry, cover it with varnish to make it nice and shiny. If you don't have varnish you can mix PVA glue with a little water instead.

Polystyrene prints

Pizza packaging is a good base for your prints.

Pretty prints, cute prints, crazy prints, funny prints – whatever mood you're in, you can create an amazing polystyrene print to match it!

A pussy cat print is a purr-fect present to give to someone special!

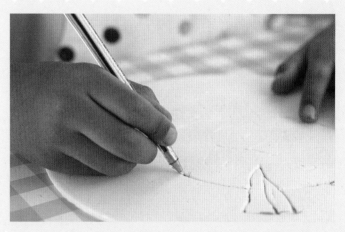

1 Draw a picture on a piece of paper with a felt-tip pen – simple designs work best. Lay it over the polystyrene and trace over the drawing with a ballpoint pen, pressing down quite hard.

2 Check that the pen indentation is fairly deep on the polystyrene. If it isn't, draw over the picture again.

4 With a roller, spread paint evenly all over your picture. Don't put too much paint on otherwise you will end up with a big splodge of paint!

5 Place coloured paper over the polystyrene and firmly press down on it with your hands.

You can print portraits of your family and friends!

3 Add texture to the polystyrene with a *ballpoint pen*. This will make your finished print more interesting!

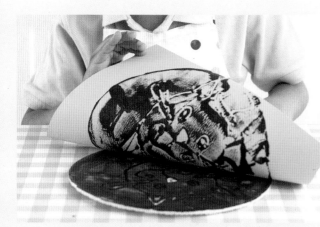

6 Carefully peel the paper off to reveal your fabulous print!

You will need:

white paper • felt-tip pen
• polystyrene packaging
• ballpoint pen • acrylic
paint • roller
• coloured paper

Plastic can be recycled easily. It can be turned into lots of things, like stuffed toys and clothing.

What is junk?

Junk is all the stuff that we throw in the bin. It could be newspapers, old clothes, or plastic bottles – junk is everywhere! But you don't need to get rid of it. Reuse your junk and turn it into something amazing.

Before you throw away that magazine, remember the "3 R's". **Reduce, reuse,** and **recycle.** If we don't recycle our junk, it gets buried in the ground or burnt, which harms the Earth's atmosphere.

Don't bin it, reuse it!

What junk can we reuse?

Fabric is fabulous. Some fabric, like wool, comes from animals. Other fabric, like lycra, is made in a laboratory. Don't throw out that old T-shirt – transform it!

Fabric

Plastic is fantastic. It is made with a substance called cellulose, which comes from the wood pulp of trees. It can take hundreds of years for plastic to disappear from the Earth – so reuse it!

Plastic

Glass

Paper

Glass is great. But the fact that it takes over one million years to break down isn't. Turn to page 60 to discover how you can reuse glass.

Paper is perfect for crafting with! Reusing paper means that fewer tress have to be cut down, saving the Earth's energy.

Metal is marvellous. It comes from rocks, which are broken up and heated, releasing the metal. Reusing metal saves the Earth from being dug up.

Metal

Reusing your junk will help **save the planet!**

49

Sammy the snake

This is Sammy the snake and he is made from egg boxes. Egg boxes can be used to make all sorts of eggcellent creatures. It's time to get cracking with this craft!

You will need:

cardboard egg boxes • scissors • green and yellow poster paint • paintbrush • skewer • embroidery needle • string • beads • red felt • PVA glue • googly eyes • two sticks

⚠️

I Ask an adult to help you cut the lids off the egg boxes and cut off each segment. You will need about 26 segments to make Sammy.

4 Thread string through one segment and tie a knot at the end of the string. Next, thread a bead onto the string, followed by another segment. Repeat with the rest of the segments.

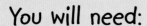

You will need about 50cm (20in) of string to make Sammy.

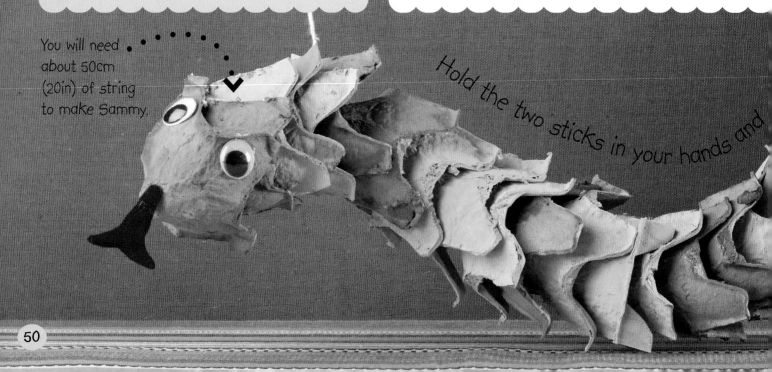

Hold the two sticks in your hands and

2 Paint 16 segments with the green poster paint and 10 segments with the yellow poster paint. Set aside to dry.

3 Ask an adult to make a hole through the middle of each segment with a skewer. Always point the skewer away from your body.

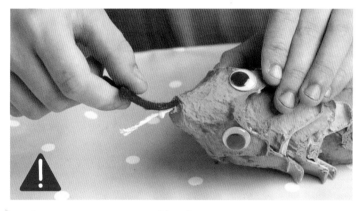

5 Leave about 3cm (1¼in) of string at the end and tie a knot. Next, give Sammy features! Cut a tongue shape out of red felt and glue onto the string. Add two googly eyes.

6 Tie two pieces of string around the top and bottom half of the snake and attach each piece of string to a stick.

make Sammy dance!

You can use cardboard, pom-poms, and garden wire to make more cute egg box critters.

51

Spoon dolly

Wooden spoons aren't just for stirring –
they can also become spectacular spoon dollies!
Gather scraps of felt, fabric, trimmings,
and sparkly sequins to decorate them.

You can craft a spoon
of someone you know,
or even one of yourself!

You will need:

tracing paper • pencil
• scissors • felt • pins
• ribbon • lace • PVA glue
• sequins • wooden spoon
• tape • pipe cleaner
• black felt-tip pen
• googly eyes

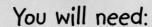

Any scraps of
colourful felt will do.

⚠️

1 Trace the felt shapes (see page 79) onto paper and cut them out. Pin the paper shapes to the felt and cut around them.

⚠️

2 Cut a piece of ribbon and lace about 12cm (5in) long and glue onto the bottom of the dress. Squirt *blobs* of glue onto the dress and stick on sequins.

3 Spread glue onto the spoon and stick on the felt hair and the front of the dress.

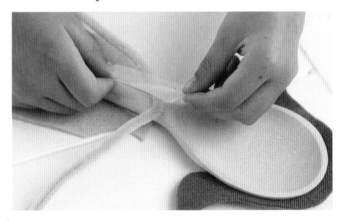

4 For the arms, cut a length of pipe cleaner about 20cm (8in) long and tape onto the back of the spoon. Then glue the back of the dress on.

5 Next, give your spoon a face! Stick on googly eyes, then draw a nose, mouth, and rosy cheeks.

6 Glue sparkly accessories onto the pipe cleaner arm and around the neck. Hook the felt handbag onto the pipe cleaner arm.

Don't throw out take-away spoons – just give them a clean and then transform them!

Use scraps of wool as hair for your spoon dollies.

Cut out felt to make cute outfits.

A cupcake case folded in half makes a pretty skirt.

Glue buttons onto a doily to make a dainty dress.

Super duper spoon show!

It's showtime! Take a look at these spoons for inspiration and make a whole cast of colourful spoons. Then put on a spectacular spoon show to entertain your family and friends.

Use frilly trimmings to make a fancy dress and feathers for a fabulous hat!

This cool lolly stick dude is wearing a sweet wrapper hat.

Make a stage to display your spoons. Wrap boxes with colourful paper and ask an adult to cut slits in the top.

Origami **boat**

These beautiful boats can be made from all types of paper, from magazines and maps, to sweet wrappers and wallpaper. Make lots of boats and then turn the page to discover what you can do with them all!

You will need:
A4 coloured or patterned paper

All aboard this brilliant boat craft!

You can make big boats, medium boats, and teeny-weeny boats!

1 Start with A4 paper, patterned or coloured side up, and fold in half.

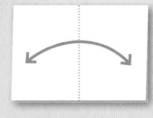

2 Fold in half again, make a crease, and then unfold.

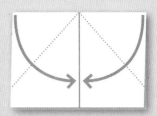

3 Fold both corners in to the centre, to make a triangle shape.

4 Fold the flap up.

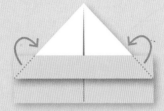

5 Fold both corners behind the triangle and then turn it over.

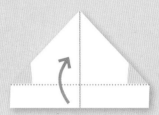

6 Fold the flap up.

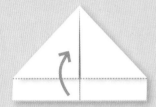

7 Poke your fingers inside to open the triangle out and then flatten down the right side, to make a diamond shape.

8 Fold the bottom point of the diamond up to the top point. Turn it over and repeat so that you have a triangle shape.

9 Poke your fingers inside to open the triangle out and then flatten down the right side, to make a diamond shape.

10 Take the upper corners of the diamond and pull them out (see the images on the right) to reveal your beautiful boat!

1 Give your origami boats more of a shape by creasing the corners and poking the underneath with your fingers, so that they can stand upright.

2 Thread about 90cm (35in) of wool through the middle of the boat and tie a knot near the end to secure it.

3 Tie another knot halfway up the wool and then thread another boat. Repeat steps 1-3 with 3 pieces of wool, threading 2 boats on each piece of wool.

4 Make a cross shape with two sticks and wrap about 240cm (94in) of wool around the middle to secure them together.

5 Next, wrap each piece of wool with the boats attached around the edges of each stick and secure with a knot.

6 To make sails, cut diamond shapes from coloured paper and fold in half. Use glue to stick the sails to the wool.

Wrap wool around the middle of the sticks and hang your mobile from a shelf.

Boat mobile

This brilliant boat mobile is the perfect way to show off your boats in all their glory!

You will need:

8 origami boats • embroidery needle • wool • scissors • 2 sturdy sticks • coloured paper • glue stick

You can also design your own boat. Use plain brown paper, garden wire, and chalk.

59

Snow globe

Raid your toy box for a plastic toy that will fit comfortably inside a glass jar and make a snow globe. It is the perfect way to display a toy treasure that you no longer play with.

Adding a teaspoon of glycerine to the water will thicken it, creating a snowfall effect with the glitter.

⚠ 1 Ask an adult to glue a pebble onto the inside of the lid to give your toy height. Glue your toy onto the pebble. If you don't want to use a pebble, glue the toy straight onto the lid. Set aside to dry.

⚠ 4 To make sure water doesn't leak out, ask an adult to spread strong glue on the inner rim of the jar lid and screw it on tightly.

Use felt that goes well with your plastic toy. This dino is surrounded by green felt that looks like grass.

You can use a photo of

2 Cut a piece of card to the length of your jar and decorate in any way you like. Cover both sides of the card with tape. Use your fingers to remove any air bubbles on the tape so that water doesn't seep through.

3 Place the card inside the jar and pour in water, almost to the top. Add a teaspoon of glycerine and a teaspoon of glitter.

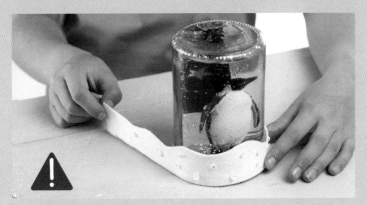

5 Cut a piece of felt to wrap around your jar. Cut curves on the top edge of the felt and glue on sequins to decorate. Glue the felt onto the jar and leave to dry.

6 Shake your jar and watch the glittery magic within!

You will need:

pebble • glass jar with lid • strong glue
• plastic toy • scissors • card • tape
• water • glycerine • glitter • felt • sequins

someone special as a background for your snow globe.

5... 4... 3... 2... 1... Blast off!

Jet pack

Do you want to blast off into space? Then you need this jet pack! Rinse out two plastic bottles, follow the steps, and get ready for a space adventure.

You will need:

red, yellow, and orange tissue paper • scissors • 2 plastic bottles • gaffer tape • cardboard • embroidery needle • elastic • black, yellow, and red electrical tape • 2 bottle tops • grey electrical tape • PVA glue

You can add more controls to your jet pack with bottle tops and bits of silver tin foil.

Get ready! Cut out 18 flame shapes, about 18cm (7in) long, from the red, yellow, and orange tissue paper.

Cut a piece of cardboard about 16cm (6½in) wide and 25cm (10in) in length.

1 Wrap 2 strips of gaffer tape around each bottle. Line up the bottles so that the strips are side-by-side. Wrap 2 strips of gaffer tape around both bottles to bind them together.

2 Cover the cardboard base with strips of gaffer tape. Ask an adult to make holes in each corner and thread elastic through the holes to make arm loops. Secure the end with a knot.

3 Lay a strip of gaffer tape about 35cm (14in) long near the bottom of the base, sticky side up. Stick it down with 2 strips of gaffer tape.

4 Place the bottles onto the base and stick both sides of the long strip of gaffer tape to the side of each bottle.

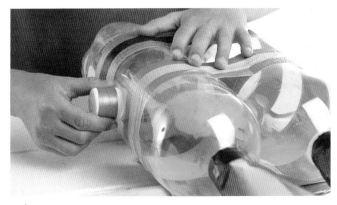

5 Lay 9 flames out and place a strip of electrical tape along the top. Then wrap the tape with the flames attached around the bottle top. Repeat with the remaining flames and the other bottle top.

6 Wrap yellow and red electrical tape around the middle of the 2 strips of gaffer tape. Then tape 2 bottle tops together with grey electrical tape and glue onto the side of the bottle.

Alien junkship

Is it a bird? Is it a plane? No, it's the amazing alien junkship! Your awesome felt aliens need an equally awesome ship to travel in. The best thing about this ship is that it's made from junk!

You will need:

strips of tin foil • scissors • plastic bottle • paper bowl • pencil • glue stick • tape • Blu-Tack™ • two felt-tip pen lids • clear dome-shaped cup lid • electrical tape • strong glue • bottle tops

See pages 70-71 to find out how to make these friendly aliens.

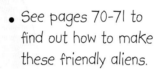

Stick a glue top onto the inside of a bottle top to make a cool control for your junkship!

You can also use a clear plastic pot if you don't have a dome-shaped cup lid.

Get ready! Cut lots of strips of tin foil to cover the edges of a paper bowl.

1 Ask an adult to cut off the bottom of a plastic bottle. Place it inside the paper bowl and draw a circle around it.

2 Ask an adult to cut out the circle. Spread the glue stick onto the strips of tin foil and stick them all around the side of the bowl.

3 Attach the bottom of the bottle to the inside of the bowl with strips of tape. Turn the bowl over.

4 Put Blu-Tack™ inside the bottle end and stick two felt-tip pen lids on it. Now your felt aliens have seats to perch on!

5 Attach the cup lid to the bowl with a strip of electrical tape on the inside and on the outside of the lid.

6 Use the strong glue to stick four bottle tops around the sides of the bowl.

7 Lastly, place two of your felt alien pals onto the pen lids inside the junkship.

Junk

Alien invasion

Felt

Felt is used to make bags, hats, and slippers because it's **strong and light.**

What is felt?

Felt is made from wool, but it isn't spun or woven like wool is, it's squashed! Felt is perfect for making crafts with because it is easy to sew and cut, and doesn't unravel.

Turn to pages 70-71 to find out how to make an awesome felt alien!

Felt is one of the oldest materials. For thousands of years it has been used to make a variety of things – from carpets and clothes, to shoes and saddles.

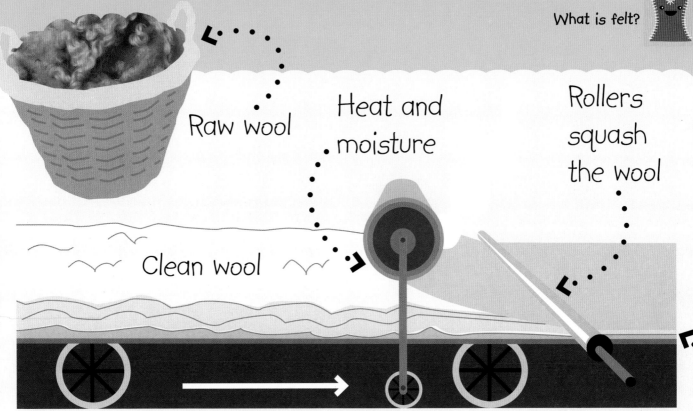

Raw wool

Heat and moisture

Rollers squash the wool

Clean wool

The wool moves along the conveyor belt.

Felt ...

How is felt made?

Raw wool is cleaned and then it goes through a machine, where heat and moisture are applied to it. Rollers squash the material flat, pressing the fibres together, producing felt.

Working with felt used to be a risky business! Hats made with felt were treated with a substance called mercury. Mercury could poison the hatmaker and cause uncontrollable shaking and loss of memory...

...and that's where the saying **"mad as a hatter"** is thought to have come from!

Felt is traditionally used to make yurts, a type of tent, because it is water-resistant, strong, and retains heat.

Awesome aliens

The felt aliens have landed on Earth! But don't worry, these friendly Martians come in peace. Use up scraps of felt to make them and then pop them on top of your pencils.

You don't have to use these exact colours of felt.

You will need:

tracing paper • pencil • scissors • coloured felt • pins • embroidery thread • needle

Make Zork's alien buddies.

Zork

Get ready! Use this template to trace Zork's felt shapes individually onto paper and cut them out.

body x 2

Actual size template

1 Pin the paper shapes onto felt and carefully cut around them.

2 Position the black circle onto the white circle, and secure to the pink body with about five stitches.

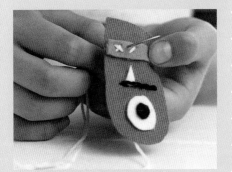

3 Sew on the tooth using two rows of backstitch (see page 80). Next, sew on the blue strip using cross-stitch (see page 80).

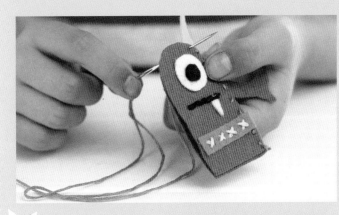

4 Start stitching around the side of the body using running stitch (see page 80). Place the arms and the ears in between the pink body pieces, and stitch them in as you go along.

5 Leave the bottom of Zork unstitched so that you can put him on top of your pencil.

They are out of this world!

Morg

Gorky

Stux

Flim

Once you have made Zork, you can create your own aliens. Use Zork's buddies as inspiration or make them as weird and wacky as you like!

Gold medal

Make this marvellous felt medal and then give it to someone special for being Number One. Or, if you've been on your best behaviour, you can wear it with pride yourself!

Use a piece of ribbon that fits comfortably around your neck.

Who will you present your gold medal to?

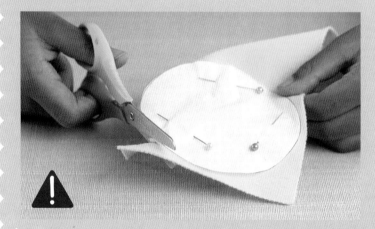

⚠️

1 Pin one circle to orange felt, one to white felt, and one to yellow felt. Pin the smaller circle to orange felt. Carefully cut around each circle.

4 Use blanket stitch (see page 80) to attach the yellow circle to the white and orange circles.

You will need:

tracing paper • pencil
• compass • scissors
• felt • pins • embroidery
needle • embroidery
thread • ribbon

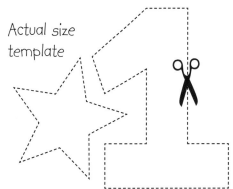

Actual size
template

Get ready! Trace these templates onto paper. Then, use a compass to draw 3 circles about 10cm (4in) in width and a smaller circle about 8cm (3in) in width onto paper. Pin each shape to felt and cut around it.

2 Use running stitch (see page 80) to sew the white number one and the white star to the orange circle.

3 Sew the orange circle to the yellow circle using running stitch.

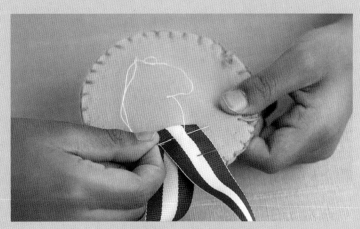

5 Cut a piece of ribbon that is long enough to go around your neck and fold it in half. Use running stitch to sew the ribbon to the back of the medal.

Once you've made the gold medal, try making this rosette or designing a badge of your own. Sew a brooch pin onto the back and pin it onto your top.

Chirp, chirp!

Bean bag **bird**

You can also use feathers to decorate your bean bags.

This bean bag bird is bags of fun to make and play with. You will need to use basic sewing skills to put it together. Then you can play catch with it, juggle it, display it, or cuddle it!

Make lots of birds in different colours and play the bean bag game on the next page.

You can glue the fabric and felt pieces to the bean bag if you don't want to use running stitch.

Get ready! For the felt rectangle body, cut a piece of felt about 20cm (8in) in width and 40cm (16in) in length.

You will need:

tracing paper • scissors • pins • coloured felt • scrap of fabric • needle • embroidery thread • rice • button

1 Trace the felt and fabric shapes (*see page 79*) onto paper and cut them out. Pin the paper shapes to the felt and fabric and cut around them.

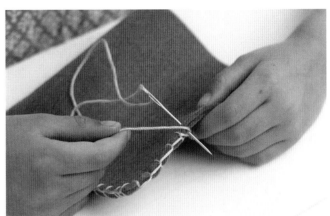

2 Fold the felt rectangle in half. Sew along one short side and the long side using *blanket stitch* (*see page 80*).

3 Carefully pour the rice into the opening, $\frac{2}{3}$ of the way to the top.

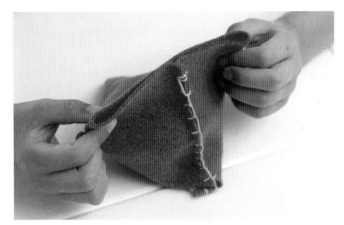

4 Pinch the sides of the opening together to make a triangle shape. Stitch along the opening using *blanket stitch*.

5 Use running stitch to sew the felt heart crest to the side of the triangle, just behind the blanket stitches near the top. For the *beak*, stitch both triangles onto the front using running stitch.

6 For the eye, sew a button onto one side of the triangle. To finish, stitch the pointed end of the fabric heart wing to the side using running stitch.

Bean bag game!

Once you have made lots of bean bag birds, you can play the bean bag game. Gather your friends and grab a basket or a bucket. Stand back from the basket and take turns to throw the bean bags in. How many bean bags can you get into the basket? The person who gets the most in wins!

Tweet, tweet!

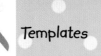
Templates

These handy templates will help you make a handful of the projects.

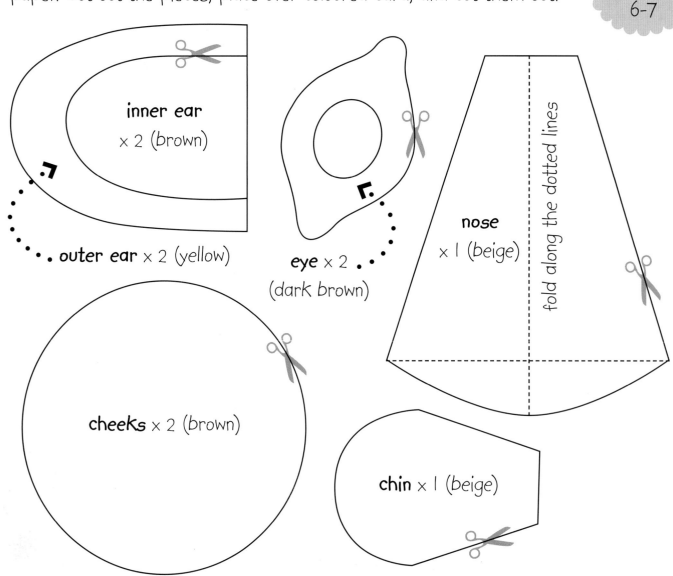

Larry the lion mask

Trace the templates for Larry the lion mask onto tracing paper. Cut out the pieces, place over coloured card, and cut them out.

Find me on pages 6-7

inner ear
x 2 (brown)

outer ear x 2 (yellow)

eye x 2
(dark brown)

nose
x 1 (beige)

fold along the dotted lines

cheeks x 2 (brown)

chin x 1 (beige)

Find me on pages 74-75

Bean bag bird

Trace the templates for the bean bag bird onto tracing paper. Cut out the pieces, then pin them to the felt and fabric before you cut them out.

fabric heart wing × 1

beak × 2

felt heart crest × 1

Spoon dolly

dress × 2

handbag strap × 1. Use glue to stick the strap to the handbag.

handbag × 1

hair × 1

Trace the templates for the spoon dolly onto tracing paper. Cut out the pieces, then pin them to the felt before you cut them out.

Find me on pages 52-53

Sewing techniques

The following stitches are used in projects throughout the book.

Running stitch

This versatile stitch is used for seams, sewing fabric together, and for making gathers.

Push the needle in and out of the fabric and pull to make a stitch.

Keep the stitches and the spaces between them small and even.

Backstitch

This is a very strong stitch. It makes a continuous line of stitches so it's best for sewing two pieces of fabric securely.

Make the stitch then bring the needle back to the place where the last stitch finished.

Bring the needle out, and begin the next stitch.

Finished stitches.

Cross-stitch

This stitch is good for adding decoration to your projects.

Make a diagonal stitch. Then make another stitch on the opposite side, to make a cross shape.

Bring the needle out, ready to begin the next stitch.

Finished stitches.

Blanket stitch

This is a good stitch for making neat, decorative edges and for sewing one piece of fabric to another.

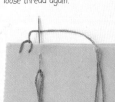

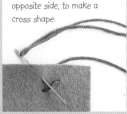

Pull the needle through the fabric. Then push the needle back through the fabric, next to the first stitch, making sure to catch the loose thread, as shown.

Push the needle up through the fabric, catching the loose thread again.

Keep the stitches neat and even.

Index

Acknowledgements

With thanks to: Jennifer Lane for additional editing, MaSovaida Morgan for assisting at a photo shoot, and Carrie Love and James Mitchem for proofreading.
With special thanks to the models: Isabella and Eleanor Moore-Smith, Cinnamon Clarke, Sol Matofska-Dyer, Miia Newman-Turner, Kaylan Patel, Isabella Thompson, Eva Menzie, Kathryn Meeker, and Jo Casey.

All images © Dorling Kindersley